Darling M̶~~~~

Through t̶~~~~
the lows ~~~~
together, love you
always, Ash xx

THE LITTLE BOOK OF
MUM

Published by OH!
20 Mortimer Street
London W1T 3JW

Text © 2021 OH!
Design © 2021 OH!

Disclaimer:

ISBN 978-1-80069-001-1

Compiled by: Victoria Godden
Editorial: Stella Caldwell
Project manager: Russell Porter
Design: Tony Seddon
Production: Rachel Burgess

A CIP catalogue record for this book is available from the British Library

Printed in Dubai

10 9 8 7 6 5 4 3 2 1

THE LITTLE BOOK OF
MUM

LITTLE WORDS OF STRENGTH, WISDOM AND LOVE

CONTENTS

INTRODUCTION - 6

8
....
CHAPTER
ONE
....
**THE BIRTH
OF A
MOTHER**

62
....
CHAPTER
TWO
....
**THE HIGHS
AND LOWS**

104

....

C H A P T E R
THREE

....

**AN
UNBREAKABLE
BOND**

162

....

C H A P T E R
FOUR

....

**MOTHER
NATURE**

INTRODUCTION

There's a reason why one of the most common "thank you" speeches at the Oscars is a winner thanking his or her mother. With the love and support of the woman who gave us life, it feels like anything might be possible.

Anyone who is a mum knows just how tough and challenging the role can be. A mother carries her child for nine months before giving birth. Then she embarks on an endless round of feeding, bathing, teaching and entertaining – and that's just the baby and toddler years! Motherhood can be overwhelming. It brings great responsibility and plenty of sleepless nights – and it's not even a paid job!

But of course, being a mum is also incredibly rewarding. The deep love a mother feels for her children and the heart-swelling pride she takes in them makes it all worthwhile. The special bond between a mother and child is like nothing else in the world, and it is something to be cherished.

Of course, a mother might know how to push her child's buttons. What she has to say might be difficult to hear sometimes, and she's bound to know plenty of embarrassing childhood stories! But a mother nurtures her children with unconditional love and support, helping them to grow wings and fly on their own. And even though everyone in the world has a mum, every mother-and-child relationship is something truly unique.

If you've been given this book by your pride and joy, you'll probably read its words with a knowing smile and fond memories. If you're about to become a mum, think of this as your introduction to the beautiful, truly life-shattering (in all senses of the word!) journey that you are about to embark on. Most of all, however, the following pages offer us all a moment to pause, celebrate, give thanks for and marvel at the magical wonder of mothers.

CHAPTER
ONE

The Birth of a Mother

Becoming a mother is one of the most magical, profound and difficult things a woman can do.

After growing and carrying your baby around for nine months, this tiny, vulnerable little bundle arrives and you suddenly have that most-revered, most-loved title of "mother".

"

Motherhood:
All love begins and
ends there.

"

Robert Browning

"

Life began
with waking up
and loving my
mother's face.

"

George Eliot

A mother's sacrifice
isn't giving birth.

It's nine months without
wine...

Our mother's voice is one of the first things we ever hear, and it's no different for birds.

It's been found that mother birds can communicate with their chicks while still in the egg, so that when they do hatch, they recognize her call.

Oxytocin, known as the love hormone, floods a mother's body during birth, reducing stress, calming her down and helping with pain during labour.

It also hangs around after birth too, helping a new mother feel more relaxed, well-nourished and bonded with her baby.

In Greek mythology,

Eileithyia

was the goddess
of childbirth.

It's
estimated
that

1 in 250

pregnancies
results in
twins.

66

If pregnancy
were a book they
would cut the last
two chapters.

99

Nora Ephron

Uplifting Birth Affirmations

Birth is the ultimate act of love.

Birth is miraculous however it happens.

Bring it on!

My baby gives me the strength to do anything.

I trust my instincts.

I fill my body and mind with good stuff.

I shake off any pressure to be perfect and simply try my best.

I am present and I am doing this.

I quiet my mind and let my body give birth.

I am strong.

66

Childbirth is
more admirable than
conquest, more amazing
than self-defence,
and as courageous as
either one.

99

Gloria Steinem

What is Hypnobirthing?

Hypnobirthing is a method of pain management that can be used during labour and birth.

It involves using a mixture of visualization, relaxation and deep breathing techniques.

There are about

2 *billion*

mothers
in the world.

"

Our birth is but a sleep and a forgetting. Not in entire forgetfulness, and not in utter nakedness, but trailing clouds of glory do we come.

"

William Wordsworth

66

When you are a mother, you are never really alone in your thoughts. A mother always has to think twice, once for herself and once for her child.

99

Sophia Loren

Things it's OK to do when you are a new mum

Not shower for two days.

Not wash your hair for a week.

Only eat carbs.

Cry for no apparent reason.

Forget about housework.

Forget what day/month/year it is.

Want some time away from
your baby.

Want to be with your baby
all the time.

Want your baby to go to sleep.

Want your baby to wake up
(because you miss them).

Take any help offered.

Let visitors make their own tea.

"

Let choice
whisper in your ear
and love murmur
in your heart.
Be ready.
Here comes life.

"

Maya Angelou

"

Think of stretch
marks as pregnancy
service stripes.

"

Joyce Armor

"

Whatever else is
unsure in this
stinking dunghill
of a world
a mother's love
is not.

"

James Joyce

"

There is no way to
be a perfect mother,
and a million ways
to be a good one.

"

Jill Churchill

5 Top Tips for new mums

Ask for help.

Build a routine.

Look after yourself – go for a walk, take a shower, drink a coffee!

Make healthy choices.

Remember that every stage is exactly that, a stage! And it won't last forever.

"

A baby fills
a place in your
heart that you never
knew was empty.

"

Anonymous

"

Being a mother has made my life complete.

"

Darcey Bussell

Today, women are nearly

31

when they first give birth,
whereas a generation ago the
average age was

24

The oldest woman to give birth was an Indian woman named *Omkari Panwar*, who delivered twins aged **72**, in June 2008.

She conceived the twins – a boy and a girl – by in vitro fertilization (IVF), and gave birth via C-section.

Source: ABC News

"

Suddenly
she was here.
And I was no longer
pregnant;
I was a mother.
I never believed in
miracles before.

"

Ellen Greene

Because one of the first utterances babies make is a "ma" sound, most languages around the world have that sound as the basis for their word for "mother".

Mum's the word

Here are some of the different words for
"mother" from around the world:

Irish: *Máthair*

Arabic: *Ahm*

German: *Mutter*

Japanese: *Okaasan* or *Haha*

Spanish: *Madre, Mama* or *Mami*

Samoan: *Tina*

Portuguese: *Mãe*

Hungarian: *Anya*

French: *Mère* or *Maman*

Swahili: *Mama*

"

Making the decision to have a child is momentous. It is to decide for ever to have your heart go walking around outside your body.

"

Elizabeth Stone

"

Ah babies. They're
more than just
adorable creatures
on whom you can
blame your farts.

"

Tina Fey

"

The two most important days in your life are the day you are born and the day you find out why.

"

Mark Twain

"

I feel whole at last.

"

Meg Mathews

Mummy bloggers to boost morale

Anna Whitehouse aka Mother Pukka
@mother_pukka

Louise Pentland @louisepentland

Candice Brathwaite @candicebrathwaite

Rosie Ramsey @rosemarinoramsey

Liv Thorne @livsalone

Giovanna Fletcher
@happymumhappybaby
and @mrsgifletcher

"

Motherhood
is the biggest
on-the-job training
scheme
in the world.

"

Erma Bombeck

"

I remember leaving the hospital thinking, 'Wait, are they just going to let me walk off with him? I don't know beans about babies. I don't have a licence to do this.'

"

Anne Tyler

66

The hand that
rocks the cradle is
the hand that rules
the world.

99

William Ross Wallace

"

The days are long but the years are short.

"

Gretchen Rubin

Mantra

I am open
to the lessons my children
teach me.

66

Parents learn a lot from their children about coping with life.

99

Muriel Spark

“

I understood once
I held a baby in my arms,
why some people
have the need to keep
having them.

”

Spalding Gray

66

Motherhood is never being number one in your list of priorities and not minding at all.

99

Jasmine Guinness

"

Motherhood is a wonderful thing. What a pity to waste it on the children.

"

Judith Pugh

The 5 types of mother

*

The Perfectionist Mother

The Unpredictable Mother

The Best Friend Mother

The Me First Mother

The Complete Mother

66

There's a lot more
to being a woman than
being a mother,
but there's a lot more
to being a mother than
most people suspect.

99

Roseanne Barr

66

Every mother leaves her footprints.

99

African proverb

A Mother's Love

Of all the special joys in life,

The big ones and the small,

A mother's love and tenderness

Is the greatest of them all.

Anon

"

You have to love your children unselfishly. That is hard. But it is the only way.

"

Barbara Bush

Mantra

I can do anything,
but I can't do everything.

"

I've begun to
love this creature
and to anticipate her
birth as a fresh twist
to a knot, which I
do not wish to untie.

"

Mary Wollestonecraft

According to Guinness World Records, the most children born to any woman in recorded history is

The mother was a peasant from Shuya, Russia, identified only as "the wife of Feodor Vassilyev".

Birthstones

January: Garnet
February: Amethyst
March: Aquamarine
April: Diamond
May: Emerald
June: Pearl and Alexandrite
July: Ruby
August: Peridot
September: Sapphire
October: Opal and Tourmaline
November: Topaz and Citrine
December: Tanzanite, Zircon
and Turquoise

66

Mother:
The most beautiful
word on the
lips of mankind.

99

Kahlil Gibran

CHAPTER
TWO

The Highs and Lows

Having children changes your life fundamentally, and with their arrival your view on the world alters forever.

They can light up your world and bring you joy like nothing else on Earth.

On the flip side, they can drive you up the wall and leave you questioning your sanity...

"

One minute you are young and cool, maybe even a little dangerous, and the next you are reading Amazon reviews for birdseed.

"

@simoncholland

Motherhood
is picking things up
off the
floor
forever.

“

Motherhood is not for the faint-hearted. Frogs, skinned knees and the insults of teenage girls are not meant for the wimpy.

”

Danielle Steele

Being a mum
means never needing
an alarm clock.

66

Sometimes the
laughter in mothering
is the recognition of the
ironies and absurdities.
Sometimes, though,
it's just pure,
unthinking delight.

99

Barbara Shapiro

66

The story of a
mother's life:
Trapped between a
scream and a hug.

99

Cathy Guisewite

THE ONLY THING KIDS WEAR OUT FASTER THAN SHOES IS PARENTS.

66

I always say
if you aren't yelling
at your kids,
you aren't spending
enough time
with them.

99

Reese Witherspoon

71

66

If evolution really
works, how come
mothers only have
two hands?

99

Ed Dussault

Mantra

Your best
is good enough.

66

Being a mom has made me so tired. And so happy.

99

Tina Fey

Kids keeping you up?
Mother killer whales don't
sleep for up to two months
after giving birth
(neither do their offspring).

earned the nickname
"Mother's Ruin"

thanks to its popularity
among women in the
mid-eighteenth century.

Mindful mum moment

Take five while you wash
your face.

Notice how the water feels when
it touches your skin. How does
the soap feel against your skin?
What does it smell like?

For those few minutes, focus
completely on the sensations of
washing your face.

Jumper

*

Definition

Something you wear
when your mother gets cold.

66

The heart of a mother
is a deep abyss
at the bottom of which
you will always find
forgiveness.

99

Honoré de Balzac

"

Hugs can do great amounts of good – especially for children.

"

Princess Diana

"

A mother's arms
are made of
tenderness and
children sleep
soundly in them.

"

Victor Hugo

Mindful mum moment

Take ten mindful breaths, inhaling for a count of five and exhaling for a count of eight.

Ten breaths will feel completely different when you take them mindfully, and they will serve as a mini-meditation experience.

66

Motherhood
has a very
humanizing effect.
Everything gets
reduced
to essentials.

99

Meryl Streep

Pause, breathe, smile

“

The world is full of
women blindsided by
the unceasing demands
of motherhood, still
flabbergasted by how
a job can be terrific
and tortuous.

”

Anna Quindlen

66

You can't scare me, I'm a mother of teenagers!

99

Unknown

"

Mothers are all
slightly insane.

"

J. D. Salinger

5 things a mum would never say

"How on earth can you see the TV sitting so far back?"

"Yeah, I used to skip school too."

"Well, if Grace's mum says it's OK, that's good enough for me."

"I don't have a tissue with me... Just use your sleeve."

"Don't bother wearing a jacket, I'm sure you'll be warm enough."

"Make Mummy a drink"

(Grapefruit and Elderflower Cocktail)

Ingredients

45 ml (1.5 oz) grapefruit vodka

15 ml (½ oz) elderflower liqueur

Squeeze of fresh lemon

90 ml (3 oz) sparkling grapefruit

Ice

Instructions

Combine vodka, elderflower liqueur and lemon juice in a cocktail shaker and shake with the ice.

Strain and top with sparkling grapefruit.

KEEP A POSITIVE MENTAL ATTITUDE

Positive affirmation

"There is
peace and love
in my home,
even in the midst
of chaos."

"

No grit, no pearl.

"

Mantra for working mums

Funniest things British mums say

I'm not your personal
taxi service.

You treat this house like a hotel!

It's like talking to a brick wall!

It'll all end in tears!

Were you born in a barn?

66

Some days I do yoga and don't yell at my kids. Some days I scream at them while eating cake over the kitchen sink. It's called balance.

99

@katiebinghamsmith

66

Children
are like crazy,
drunken,
small people in
your house.

99

Julie Bowen

Forget dad jokes...

Here are some mum puns to get you through the day

Why did the baby strawberry cry? Because his mum was in a jam!

What did the mama tomato say to the baby tomato? Catch up!

What kind of sweets do astronaut mums like? Mars bars.

Why is a computer so smart? Because it listens to its motherboard.

Silence is golden, unless you have kids, then silence is suspicious.

6 great mums in popular culture

J.K. Rowling wrote the first four *Harry Potter* books as a single mother.

Diana, Princess of Wales, mother to Princes William and Harry, famously used her status as a royal figure to support and highlight the work done by children's charities.

Marie Curie, one of the first recognized female scientists in the early 20th century, and winner of two Nobel Prizes, secured most of her achievements while raising two daughters alone.

Is there a more inspirational mother in the world than **HRH Queen Elizabeth II**? Raising four children while leading a country? Easy peasy!

Michelle Obama, self-confessed mom-in-chief, made no secret of the fact that her two daughters would always be her priority even when she stepped into the role of First Lady.

Maya Angelou became a single mother to her son, Guy, at just 17. She went on to become a renowned memoirist, novelist, educator, dramatist, producer, actress, historian, filmmaker and civil rights activist.

Recipe

Mum's iced coffee

*

Have kids.

Make coffee.

Forget you made coffee.

Drink it cold.

66

Children seldom
misquote you.
They more often repeat
word for word
what you shouldn't
have said.

99

Mae Maloo

"

At the end of the day, my most important job is still mom-in-chief.

"

Michelle Obama

"

Don't call me
an icon.
I'm just a mother
trying to help.

"

Princess Diana

CHAPTER
THREE

An Unbreakable Bond

There is nothing like a
mother's love. It is a love so
powerful that it can leave you
feeling invincible!

Mothers are our teachers,
our leaders, our protectors,
our cheerleaders
and our champions.

66

What is learnt in the cradle lasts until the grave.

99

African proverb

Life doesn't come
with a manual,
it comes
with a

mother

"

A mother's love for
her child is like nothing else
in the world.
It knows no law, no pity.
It dares all things and
crushes down remorselessly
all that stands in its path.

"

Agatha Christie

In 2014, you might have heard the gorgeous story of a cat unexpectedly mothering a clutch of ducklings.

The cat had recently given birth and when the ducklings hatched soon after, instead of seeing them as prey, she incorporated the fluffy newcomers into her own brood.

8 best qualities of a mother

Patience

Strength

Empathy

Respect

Authority

Support

Love

Kindness

"

The best
place to cry is on a
mother's arms.

"

Jodi Picoult

66

She discovered with
great delight that one does not
love one's children just because
they are one's children but
because of the friendship formed
while raising them.

99

Gabriel García Márquez

"

Mother love
is the fuel that enables
a normal
human being to do
the impossible.

"

Marion C. Garretty

"

There is only one pretty child in the world, and every mother has it.

"

Chinese proverb

66

Sooner or later
we all quote
our mothers.

99

Bern Williams

66

All I know is that I carried you
for nine months. I fed you, I
clothed you, I paid for your college
education. Friending
me on Facebook seems like a small
thing to ask in return.

99

Jodi Picoult

"

Giving advice comes
naturally to mothers.
Advice is in the genes
along with blue eyes
and red hair.

"

Lois Wyse

“

My mother taught me to walk proud and tall 'as if the world was mine'.

”

Sophia Loren

66

A mother is the truest friend we have,
when trials heavy and sudden, fall upon
us... [she will] endeavour by her kind
precepts and counsels to dissipate the
clouds of darkness, and cause peace to
return to our hearts.

99

Washington Irving

Mum-to-mum advice

If you do
what you've always
done, you'll get
what you've always
gotten.

10 "Mumisms"
(classic mum phrases)

Wear a coat!

One day you'll thank me.

I'm going to count to three.

I said, "No!"

I'm not going to repeat myself.

Ask your father.

You will always be my baby.

I will always love you, no matter what.

Because I said so.

Go play outside, it's a beautiful day!

"

Alone a child runs fast, with a mother slow, but together they go far.

"

African proverb

66

All mothers
are working
mothers.

99

Unknown

"

I want my children
to have all the things
I couldn't afford.
Then I want to move in
with them.

"

Phyllis Diller

66

There were times
when I didn't have a lot
of friends. But my mom
was always my friend.
Always.

99

Taylor Swift

"

The older I get
the more of
my mother I see
in myself.

"

Nancy Friday

66

Yes, Mother.
I can see you are flawed.
You have not hidden it.
That is your
greatest gift to me.

99

Alice Walker

"

I remember my mother's prayers and they have always followed me. They have clung to me all my life.

"

Abraham Lincoln

"

The strength of
a mother is in
the ears and on
the lips.

"

Mali proverb

It's spicy!

Universal Mum Code for

"I don't want to share".

"

God could not
be everywhere
so he
created mothers.

"

Proverb

"

To describe my
mother would be to
write about
a hurricane in its
perfect power.

"

Maya Angelou

66

I love being a mother...
I am more aware.
I feel things on a deeper
level. I have a kind of
understanding about my
body, about being
a woman.

99

Shelley Long

66

Motherhood
is mind-blowing.

99

Britney Spears

66

Once you become a
mother, your heart is no
longer yours...
My daughter is the
greatest thing I'll ever do
in my life.

99

Kim Basinger

"

My daughter thinks I'm nosy. At least that's what she says in her diary.

"

Sally Poplin

"

Oh my son's my son
till he gets him a wife.
But my daughter's my
daughter all her life.

"

Dinah Maria Mulock Craik

66

There is a point when
you aren't as much mom
and daughter as you
are adults and friends.
It doesn't happen for
everyone – but it did
for Mom and me.

99

Jamie Lee Curtis

66

A mother is a daughter's best friend.

99

Unknown

"

A man loves his sweetheart the most, his wife the best, but his mother the longest.

"

Irish proverb

66

I got it from
my mama.

99

Will.i.am

7 types of mother/ daughter relationships

The Sisters

The Role Reversal

The Strangers

The Mismatch

The Best Friends

The Ambitious and the Executor

The Authoritarian and
the Submissive

"

My mother is a
walking miracle.

"

Leonardo DiCaprio

66

All women become
like their mothers.
That is their tragedy.
No man does.
That's his.

99

Oscar Wilde

66

Sons are the anchors of a mother's life.

99

Sophocles

66

All I am I owe to my mother.

99

George Washington

❝

Men are what their mothers made them.

❞

Ralph Waldo Emerson

"

My mother had a
great deal of trouble
with me, but I think
she enjoyed it.

"

Mark Twain

66

My mother never gave up
on me. I messed up in
school so much they were
sending me home,
but my
mother sent me
right back.

99

Denzel Washington

"

Who's a boy gonna talk to if not his mother?

"

Donald E. Westlake

"

Your most valuable
parenting skill is
learning to manage
yourself first.

"

Dr Laura Markham

5 amazing things mums do and rarely get thanked for

Wipe bottoms, noses and anything else without blinking an eye!

Survive on little sleep.

Know where everything is.

Clean up constantly.

Pack a bag for a day out (water bottle, snacks, wipes, change of clothes, toys, nappies...)

66

Everything I am
or ever hope to be,
I owe to
my angel mother.

99

Abraham Lincoln

10 iconic mothers in literature

Molly Weasley
(*Harry Potter*, J.K. Rowling)

Marmee
(*Little Women*, Louisa May Alcott)

Mother (*The Railway Children*,
Edith Nesbit)

Moominmamma
(*The Moomins*, Tove Jansson)

Ma
(*Room*, Emma Donoghue)

Grandmamma
(*The Witches*, Roald Dahl)

Catelyn Stark (*Game of Thrones*,
George R. R. Martin)

Mrs Bennet (*Pride and Prejudice*,
Jane Austen)

Marilla Cuthbert (*Anne of Green
Gables*, L. M. Montgomery)

Mrs Murry (*A Wrinkle in Time*,
Madeleine L'Engle)

"

Who ran to help me
when I fell,
And would some pretty
story tell,
Or kiss the place to
make it well?
My mother.

"

Ann Taylor

One of the most interesting mothers in literary history is Grendel's mother from *Beowulf.* She attacks Beowulf's army to avenge the death of her soŋ, the monster Grendel.

"

I love my mother
for all the times
she said absolutely
nothing.

"

Erma Bombeck

“

My mother was
the one constant in my life.

”

Barack Obama

66

As long as a woman
can look ten years
younger than
her daughter, she is
perfectly satisfied.

99

Oscar Wilde

66

That dear octopus
from whose
tentacles
we never
quite escape,
nor in our
innermost
hearts
never
quite wish to.

99

Dodie Smith

CHAPTER
FOUR

Mother Nature

Mother's Day is a wonderful time to pause and celebrate our lovely mums!

The accomplishments of human mothers are amazing, and maternal instinct is one of nature's most uncompromising laws.

Sunshine

My mother, my friend so dear,

Throughout my life you're
always near.

A tender smile to guide my way,

You're the sunshine to light
my day.

Anon

"

Of all the rights of women, the greatest is to be a mother.

"

Lyn Yutang

In the UK and Ireland, Mothering Sunday, or Mother's Day, always falls on the fourth Sunday in Lent, and has been celebrated since the Middle Ages.

Mother's Day
is celebrated on the
second Sunday
in May in several
countries including
the USA, Canada,
New Zealand and
Australia.

Top 10 movies for Mother's Day

The Parent Trap (1961 or 1998)

Mamma Mia! (2008)

Steel Magnolias (1989)

Freaky Friday (1976 or 2003)

Terms of Endearment (1983)

Stepmom (1998)

Postcards from the Edge (1990)

Lion (2016)

The Sound of Music (1965)

Lady Bird (2017)

Mother's Day
is celebrated in
46 countries
around the world.

When, in 1914, American president Woodrow Wilson made Mother's Day an official holiday, the resolution declared:

"The American mother is doing so much for the home, for moral uplift, and religion, hence so much for good government and humanity."

Australians
spend an estimated
$200 million
on flowers
for Mother's Day.

Pink carnations are the flowers that represent a mother's love.

66

Who built the
drum knows best
what's inside.

99

Burundi proverb

In Norway, Mother's Day
is always on the
second Sunday in February,
Russia celebrates it on
the last Sunday in
November, and in
Indonesia, it's celebrated
on 22 December.

66

A mother is a
mother still, the
holiest thing alive.

99

Samuel Taylor Coleridge

66

Biology is the least of what makes someone a mother.

99

Oprah Winfrey

The mother who
gives birth to
the largest baby on Earth is
a mother elephant.

After enduring
22 MONTHS
of pregnancy,
she will give birth to a
90KG/200LB
calf.

Female emperor penguins
leave their egg with
the male to go out in search
of food.

They travel up to
50 MILES/80 KM
to reach the ocean and fish,
returning to regurgitate
the food for the
newly hatched chicks.

Mothers
with
teenagers
know
why animals
eat their
young.

A record-breaking feat of mothering
endurance was reported in July 2014
when scientists observed a female
deep-sea octopus brooding her eggs for
four and a half years.

Source: BBC News

During the first two years of an orangutan's life, the young rely entirely on their mothers for both food and transportation.

The mums stay with their young for

6–7 YEARS.

Furthermore, female orangutans are known to visit their mothers until they're

15 or 16.

Elephants live
in a matriarchal society.
Females in the herd
will teach a newborn calf
how to nurse.

66

Sometimes
the strength of
motherhood is
greater than
natural laws.

99

Barbara Kingsolver

66

Children reinvent the world for you.

99

Susan Sarandon

Shortest Mother's Day poem

*

You're my mother,
I would have no other!

Forest Houtenschil

In 1920, the government of France began awarding medals to mothers of large families in gratitude for their help in rebuilding the population after so many lives were lost in World War I.

Each October, Hindus honour Durga, the goddess of mothers, during the ten-day festival known as Durga Puja.

Mother's Day is one of the biggest days for flower sales in the USA.

It is also the day on which the most long-distance phone calls are made.

Around
30 million
cards are sent on
Mother's Day
in the UK.

In Thailand,
Mother's Day is
celebrated on
12 August, the
birthday of
Queen Sirikit.

66

I am sure if the
mothers of various
nations could meet,
there would be no
more wars.

99

E. M. Forster

"

It will be gone
before you know it.
The fingerprints
on the wall appear
higher and higher.
Then suddenly
they disappear.

"

Dorothy Evslin